IMAGES
of America

THE LOWER
MOUNT
WASHINGTON
VALLEY

ALBANY – TAMWORTH – OSSIPEE

TAMWORTH: This small open stage transported summer visitors on local sightseeing trips around the turn of the century. (Courtesy Tamworth Historical Society.)

IMAGES
of America

THE LOWER
MOUNT
WASHINGTON
VALLEY
ALBANY – TAMWORTH – OSSIPEE

Jean Ulitz and Mabel Hidden

ARCADIA

First published 1996
Copyright © Jean Ulitz and Mabel Hidden, 1996

ISBN 0-7524-0275-7

Published by Arcadia Publishing,
an imprint of the Chalford Publishing Corporation
One Washington Center, Dover, New Hampshire 03820
Printed in Great Britain

Library of Congress Cataloging-in-Publication Data applied for

Dedicated to my friend and co-author
Mabel Hidden (1919–1996)

Contents

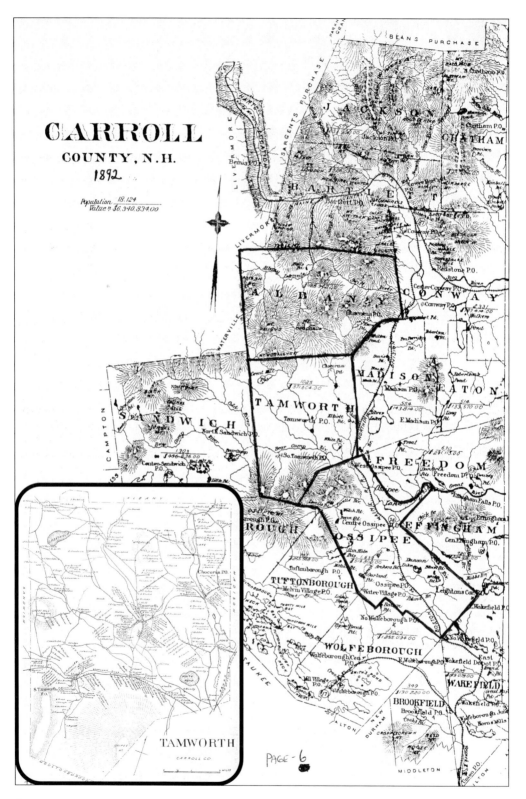

CARROLL

COUNTY, N.H.
1892

Population 18,124
Value $6,340,834.00

TAMWORTH

CARROLL CO.

PAGE-6

Introduction

The Lower Mt. Washington Valley developed a unique history as Albany, Tamworth, and Ossipee, three towns with many of the same needs and opportunities, bonded together. None became high-powered manufacturing or logging centers; all built small mills to provide for the daily needs of their own people. All needed water and water was abundant. The breath-taking scenery drew an ever-increasing influx of people—not immigrants from Europe, but mostly English settlers from Massachusetts and Connecticut, who came via the "Better Route" through the valley, looking for new land, new hope, and a new life. Lodging grew at a rapid pace; transportation became, if not plush, far above the usual rough-and-ready bone shakers. Ossipee, on its way to becoming the county center of law and order, brought the railroad, a prime move in expansion. Albany capitalized on its pristine wilderness and scenery. Tamworth, central in the valley chain, offered innumerable accommodations from small farm-style inns to huge hotels. The combination of comfort and scenic beauty brought such notables as President Grover Cleveland and family, Professor William James, Professor John Finley and family, John Greenleaf Whittier, and many more. The three towns are anchored by beautiful Mt. Chocorua. Albany owns the mountain, Tamworth "owns" the world-famous view, and Ossipee's Jewell Hill and Boulder Hill provide a grand look at the mountaintop while driving north on Route 16. One also catches sightings of majestic Mt. Washington along this stretch of the state road.

Ossipee, with lovely Ossipee Lake, the Bearcamp River, and many fine streams and ponds, must have been an appealing area for settlers. Originally known as "Ko-Was-Ki-Ki" (meaning "pine tree") by local Indians, the town was incorporated February 22, 1785, as Ossipee. Seeing the commercial needs of the valley, Ossipee produced large mills and stores, and most importantly, brought the railroad. Several distinct neighborhoods developed: Ossipee Corner, with the county courthouse and other branches of government; Center Ossipee (originally Mt. View), home of the *Carroll County Independent*, a weekly newspaper established in 1881 and moved from Effingham in the 1920s; and West Ossipee, with the major railroad station bringing Frankson's Furniture Factory, White's Garage, stores, homes, and train loads of visitors. Moultonville, Chickville, and Roland Park are also among the small communities still holding to their identities and churches. These satellite villages are common to the local scene in the state. Lack of transportation formed them; culture and habit maintain them.

Tamworth was chartered on October 14, 1766, by Benning Wentworth. The central link in the three-town chain, it was settled along the Swift River for water power. Dozens of small mills sprang up—sawmills, shingle mills, clapboard mills, nail makers, and on and on. As the railroad brought more and more visitors, the town gradually eased out of the mill business and into the lodging business. The exquisite view of Mt. Chocorua towering over Chocorua Lake was, and still is, an irresistible magnet for tourists. Boarding houses, inns, and hotels proliferated with the help of Ossipee's railroad. Many of the visiting families continued through the years, their descendants becoming full-time residents. The big farms with sheep and cattle have given way to "current use" as citizens work to keep Tamworth beautiful. A few have allowed small developments. The town is made up of five parts—Tamworth Village (the largest), Chocorua Village, South Tamworth, Whittier, and Wonalancet—each with its own character, church, and culture, fiercely clung to even today. Tamworth was named for Tamworth, England, which was in turn named for the Viscount Tamworth, a renowned military man.

At the top of the chain is Albany, with its deep woods, fresh flowing streams, challenging mountains, and numerous ponds (the largest being Whitton of 105 acres and Iona Lake with over 74 acres), making it an outdoorsman's paradise. Albany's inner woodlands need to be experienced to be appreciated; the scenery is spectacular, and as a result Albany's fine hotels flourished. Tucked away in some of the valleys are nice old farms still owned by descendants of Albany pioneers. On August 28, 1882, residents of Albany, along with Tamworth and other towns, watched Mt. Chocorua turn into a "towering inferno" as fire, started by a careless traveler, raced to the top of the mountain. The scar lasted for many years. Albany has always had strong ties to Tamworth with family and friends in Pequaket and Chocorua Village. The name of Indian Chief Chocorua is legend in both towns. Albany began on November 6, 1766, as Burton, when Royal Governor of NH Benning Wentworth granted some 20,000 acres of land to be developed. The name was later changed to Albany and incorporated on July 2, 1833. The town is 85 percent National Forest. The people are hard working, extremely interested in their town, and they run the town government with enthusiasm. Several businesses stretch along Route 16, including restaurants, a motel, small garages, gift shops, a lakeside campground, and the famous World Fellowship Center just off Route 16. Business is evident but not intrusive to the eye. A quiet, small town, Albany continues as it always has, with industrious citizens, beautiful scenery, and a way of life almost anyone could envy.

TAMWORTH: Reverend Samuel Hidden, the first minister of the congregation, served from 1792 to 1837. After the old Meeting House became the Town House, this imposing Congregational church was built in 1853. David Ruell in his survey called it "one of the best mid 19th century churches in the Lakes Region . . . the fine workmanship, good proportions of design and height of the belfry tower give the church an impressive dignity that raises it above the average church of the period and region . . ." The little building to the left was a shoe shop owned by a Newell Burleigh but nothing remains of it today. (Courtesy Millie Streeter.)

One
Readin', Writin', and Prayin'

Libraries, schools, and churches have been, and probably always will be, the social as well as the educational, intellectual, and religious link in the lives of the valley citizens. Tamworth had the third earliest social library in the state, founded in 1796. Today Tamworth has two libraries open to the public; Albany has none, but Ossipee opened the Lord Memorial Library in 1939. One-room schoolhouses were once plentiful and played an important part of life in the valley. Religion, too, has always had a significant role in the life of the local people: Albany had one church; Tamworth had seven at one time, six today; and Ossipee has had seventeen different churches over the years—it now has eight, with three other church buildings in Granite and Chickville holding annual services.

CHOCORUA: Chocorua Public Library, founded in 1888, was funded by subscription, supported by contributions, and was later privately endowed. It was first housed at the village post office until Runnells Hall (above) was constructed in 1897 with a room set aside for the library. In 1968, in conjunction with Runnells Hall Trustees (who provided the land), the Library Trustees provided the money to raze the old building and to erect the present-day library and hall. (Courtesy Cook Memorial Library.)

TAMWORTH: The public library in Tamworth was established in 1892, and was housed in a small space at the Town House until this lovely building was constructed in 1895 in memory of Charles Cook, a local storekeeper and legislator, by his widow. As Ruell said in his *A Guide to National Register Properties in the Lakes Region*: "The result was one of the state's most attractive late 19th century libraries, an exuberantly Victorian building." In 1980 the Cook Memorial Library was entered in the National Register of New Hampshire Historic Places. In 1981 the building was enlarged and rededicated. (Courtesy Millie Streeter.)

CENTER OSSIPEE: A public library was first established in 1899 in a house across from the present library and then moved to the Community House at the site of the present elementary school. In 1939, on land deeded to the town by Frank Lord, his two sisters built the Lord Memorial Library (above) in his memory. In 1989–90, a 3,600-square-foot addition was completed. (Courtesy Ossipee Historical Society.)

ALBANY: Located on Route 16, the Lords Mill School (*c.* 1900) closed in 1945—the last of Albany's one-room schoolhouses. The building is now the Golden Age Shop. (Courtesy R. and G. Morrill.)

ALBANY: The Birch Intervale School was built in Wonalancet in 1894 for $300. Pupils in this 1940s picture were doing a history project on one-room schoolhouses while attending a private Wonalancet school. From left to right are: (front) Gilbert Collins; (middle row) Joanne Read Floyd, the Mather twins, and Judy King; (back row) Ethel Berry (teacher), Shirley Roberts Eldridge, Dorothy Roberts, Ann McKee, Bruce Bowles, and Francis Wacker. The building eventually burned. (Courtesy David Bowles.)

ALBANY: These schoolchildren (c. 1930) are, from left to right: (front row) Charles Hodgdon, Sarah Pennell, Dorothea Moore, Irma Morrill, Edwin Pennell, and Alfred Bell; (middle row) Richard Lane, Harold Brown, and Norman Bell; (back row) Almee White Morrill (teacher), Harry Moore, Richard Brown, and Basil Bell. (Courtesy G. and R. Morrill.)

ALBANY: Students of the Lords Mill School in 1943 hold an afghan made for the war effort. (Courtesy G. and R. Morrill.)

OSSIPEE: The postcard says "Ossipee Schoolhouse" with no location or year. Opinions differ as to its identification but it serves as an excellent example of a one-room school in Ossipee in the 1800s. (Courtesy Steve Damon.)

CHICKVILLE: Unfortunately these children with faces so somber and serious cannot be identified nor the date verified in this scene at the Chickville School. (Courtesy Ossipee Historical Society.)

CENTER OSSIPEE: The Ossipee Center School existed from 1884 to 1924. It is now the parish hall of the First Congregational Church. (Courtesy Ossipee Historical Society.)

CENTER OSSIPEE: The Ossipee Central School was built in 1925. The old part (right) was razed; the 1964 addition on the left has been incorporated into the new school, built in the 1990s. (Courtesy Ossipee Historical Society.)

TAMWORTH: The Stevenson School on Cleveland Hill Road was moved to the other side of the road and used as a study by Professor John Finley. In 1865 Martha Boyden taught here; other teachers were Edna Cummings Mason, Alice Hoag, Amy Hoag Boyden, and stern Mabel Quimby. Pupils Marian Spaulding and Evelyn Spaulding Wallace traveled to school by horse and wagon (horse and sleigh in winter). Other pupils were the Grace and Clark children and Fred Tewksbury. (Courtesy Cook Memorial Library.)

TAMWORTH: Susan Kingsbury taught at the Pease Hill School. The building is privately owned today by the Larrivee family. (Courtesy Cook Memorial Library.)

CHOCORUA: Attendees at the Pequaket School (c. 1905) are, from left to right: (front) Norman Nickerson; (middle row) Paul Schoolcraft, Hattie Nickerson, Nellie Moore, Axie Schoolcraft, Arthur Frost, Sadie Frost, Alice Schoolcraft, and Richard Moore; (back row) Edith Nickerson, Frank Moore, the teacher (who proved impossible to identify), Winfield Nickerson, Irene Frost, and William Down. (Courtesy Cook Memorial Library.)

TAMWORTH: The Village School was built around 1908, with grades one through four taught on the left side of the building and grades five through eight on the right. When the new Brett School was built in 1956, the high schoolers went to Conway. John and Mabel Hidden bought the building in 1959 and it housed the post office, laundry, pre-school, and barber shop, as well as serving as a residence. Since 1995 Tamworth Family Practice has owned and occupied the renovated space. (Courtesy Steve Damon.)

16

TAMWORTH: At this time (c. 1931) the Village School offered two years of high school. The pupils are, from left to right: (front row) Herbert Levitt, Howard Grace, Ray Davis, and John Hidden; (middle row) Evelyn Wiggin Racine, Melba Smith, Ada Leach, Phyllis Green, Charlotte Hammond, and Thelma Watson; (back row) Hook Welch, Carroll Grace, Osmond Hatch (teacher), Ruth Berry, and Agnes Johnson. (Courtesy J. and M. Hidden.)

TAMWORTH: Village School students in the 1930s. From left to right are: (front row) Viola Eldridge, Eileen Bodge, Beatrice Welch, Laura Osgood, and Betty Bickford; (back row) Bertha Robinson, Ralph Trask, Louis Copper, Robert Trask, Bernard Hutchins, Lawrence Brett, Hazen Eldridge, Teddy Smalley, and Helen Welch. (Courtesy Cook Memorial Library.)

SOUTH TAMWORTH: These pupils at the Bennett's Corner School (*c.* 1932) are, from left to right: (front row) Edna Hutchins, Richard Mason, and Arthur Mason; (middle row) Ross Kiersted, Helen Brown, Christina Hutchins, and Don Hutchins; (back row) three unknown boys, Paul Hutchins, Virginia Bookholz, Victoria Mason Brett, unknown, and Marguerite Sweet. (Courtesy Elva Bickford.)

SOUTH TAMWORTH: Students at the Bemis School in 1940. From left to right are: (front row) Leland Whiting, Philip Ames, Charles Ames, Danny Hayford, Marilyn Larribee Evans, and Robert Floyd; (back row) Priscilla Stacey, Don Leach, Ethel Ames, Wesley Ames, Maude Gordon, and Joe Baker. (Courtesy Union Hall Association.)

GRANITE: The Early Settlers Meeting House was built before 1812 on land donated by Jacob Leighton. It still stands today at Leighton's Corner in Granite. In 1928 the rights to the building were assigned to the Ossipee Historical Society and in turn the Society has kept the building in repair and has held annual services. (Courtesy Ossipee Historical Society.)

CENTER OSSIPEE: The First Congregational Church was built in 1828–29. The first regular pastor was Reverend Samuel Arnold, who was installed by a council headed by Reverend Samuel Hidden of Tamworth. (Courtesy Ossipee Historical Society.)

WHITTIER: The St. Andrews in the Valley Episcopal Church held a groundbreaking ceremony in 1919, laid the cornerstone in 1923, and had the building consecrated in 1927 on land given by Ida Berry on old Route 25. Walter Kilham designed this lovely building; the contractor was Charles Smart; the stone mason was Ernest Mason; and the first minister was Reverend Frederick Cowper. In his survey, David Ruell called the church a "well preserved example of early 20th century Gothic Revival." Today its parishioners consist of not only Tamworth citizens but also residents from surrounding towns, and it is an active force in community service. (Courtesy Florence Fortier.)

CHOCORUA: The Our Lady of Perpetual Help Catholic Church was built c. 1901 as a summer mission chapel on land given by the Hayford family to the Roman Catholic Diocese. At some time between 1906 and 1949 the church was either remodeled extensively or rebuilt. It has been said that it burned and was rebuilt sometime in the 1920s or '30s but no records seem to exist to confirm either speculation. Ruell described it as "a pleasant building with some interesting Gothic Revival features, the arched windows, the heavy timber and stone entry porch, the board doors with their ornate hinges and the needlelike spire." Today it is a mission church of the St. Joseph Church in Ossipee and weekly Mass is offered. (Courtesy Steve Damon.)

SOUTH TAMWORTH: The Methodist Episcopal Church (now called the South Tamworth United Methodist Church) was organized in 1824. The church building was built in 1832; in 1860 it was enlarged and a belfry and bell added. In a 1950s interview Mrs. Ernest Mason said "It used to have box stoves on each side of the door and high back pews." (Courtesy Union Hall Association.)

CHOCORUA: The Freewill Baptist Church (now called the Chocorua Community Church) was founded in 1781 but a church was not constructed until 1835. According to the *Carroll County History* the present building was erected and dedicated in 1885. There were various preachers until John Runnells came and stayed as minister for about thirty-seven years—one of the longest pastorates in the denomination. (Courtesy Cook Memorial Library.)

21

WONALANCET: The Wonalancet Union Chapel (*c.* 1907) was built in 1880 on land given by Hi and Benjamin Currier and Daniel Tilton. In 1890, when Kate Sleeper wanted the chapel restored, Hill and Waddell Mill contributed the sawing and the mill crews their time. In 1896 a tower and bell were added. In 1937 the chapel was remodeled according to the plans of architect Stanley Orcutt. David Ruell believed this was "a charming example of Colonial Revival Religious Architecture." The chapel—with summertime services—remains today a beautiful sight across the field as you enter the intervale (see p. 122). (Courtesy Steve Damon.)

ALBANY: Records for the Freewill Baptist Church date from 1811 but the chapel was not built until 1889 in South Albany. Regular services eventually became occasional. In 1931 the remaining members of the Albany church gave the building to the town to be used for town meetings and other town activities. (Courtesy Elaine Wales.)

Two

From Shank's Mare
to Four-on-the-Floor

The progression from shank's mare (an old expression for your own two feet) to riding horses, buggies, and coaches, to traveling by train, and then, by four-on-the-floors (more or less modern for fast cars) meant more tourists had access to the area in all seasons. Accompanying and complementing this growth were stores, tearooms, restaurants, post offices, and service businesses of all kinds.

TAMWORTH: The Tamworth/West Ossipee stagecoach (c. early 1900s) discharges its passengers after a run from the West Ossipee depot. Behind the coach is the Tamworth Congregational Church. The small building to the left (now long gone) was a shoe shop run by Newell Burleigh. The house to the rear of the shop was moved by Newton Kimball to Route 113-A for his daughter, Clara Kimball Black. (Courtesy Tamworth Historical Society.)

SOUTH TAMWORTH: Clint Mason, foreman of the South Tamworth Industries Furniture factory, drives the Bemis family aboard the sledge called the "sightseeing bus" back to the train depot in West Ossipee after a weekend in South Tamworth (1916). This is the state road Route 25 with the Bearcamp River in the background. (Courtesy Kate Thompson.)

SOUTH TAMWORTH: This snow roller, used to pack winter roads for travel, was hauled by three pair of oxen guided by the driver in front of the roller. Summer storage for the roller was in the barn on Sumner Clark's farm on Mountain Road. (Courtesy Kate Thompson.)

TAMWORTH: President Grover Cleveland had this road built further from his house and straighter than the original road barely indicated at the left. The Memorial Wall along this road was constructed after his death at the urging and with the fund-raising of John Finley in 1910. According to Francis Cleveland, Hi Mason was in charge of building the wall. (Courtesy Steve Damon.)

OSSIPEE: This was a favorite "watering hole" stop at the old trough on Route 28 to cool the horses on the long hot drive between Wolfeboro and Ossipee. (Courtesy Steve Damon.)

MOUNTAINVIEW: The B & M Railway Station (*c.* 1875) still stands today as Veronica Rogers' restaurant Chat and Chew. (Courtesy Ossipee Historical Society.)

MOUNTAINVIEW: O.L. and C.A. White's store is at the center with the edge of the railroad depot showing at the right in this late 1800s view. The Mountainview Post Office is in the left section of the store. It's been said that when the Democrats were in office, the post office was here; when the Republicans won out, it was at Dr. Hodsdon's Drug Store at the left rear. (Courtesy Steve Damon.)

MOUNTAINVIEW: J.W. Chamberlain's feed store and grain elevator operated until after World War II. It became Hickey's I.G.A. grocery store in 1965. In recent years it has housed various organizations. (Courtesy Steve Damon.)

OSSIPEE: Charles H. Carter's store stood to the left of the courthouse before it burned *c.* 1915. (Courtesy Beryl Kramer.)

OSSIPEE VILLAGE: Newell Sias' store, shown here at turn of the century, was destroyed by fire c. 1909. The Moulton store replaced it in 1910 and it still serves today at Ossipee Village. (Courtesy Beryl Kramer.)

WEST OSSIPEE: Smith, Parker and Company ran this general store and post office in the early part of the century. In the 1930s it was called Mt. Whittier store and run by Ned Coughlin. The Tice family owned it before it burned in the 1970s. (Courtesy Elaine Wales.)

WEST OSSIPEE: The Valley Inn Tearoom was a popular meeting place for afternoon tea in the 1930s. The building on Route 16 is a furniture store today. (Courtesy Beryl Kramer.)

CHOCORUA: One of several tearoom/gift shops in the area, the Wayside Tearoom (c. 1930s) was moved during the relocation of Route 16 in 1937. The building is now owned by Bill Carr. (Courtesy Steve Damon.)

WONALANCET: The Antlers was built by Arthur Walden (of sled dog fame) and is constructed of heavy logs flattened only on the inside and mortised at the corners. A two-story building, it housed the Antlers Tearoom and Gift Shop, the post office, and was the residence of Winifred Alexander, owner of the shop. It is now a private residence. (Courtesy Steve Damon.)

CHOCORUA: The Pascoes owned the Riverside Tearoom on the banks of the Chocorua River. It was torn down to make room for the rerouting of Route 16. (Courtesy Steve Damon.)

SOUTH TAMWORTH: Leafy Mason sits on the porch of the E.L. Mason store sometime before 1916. Homemade ice cream and root beer were the first items sold at the store; groceries were added later. The sign reads: "root beer, cigars, broilers, new potatoes, onions, cucumbers, cabbage, new beets." (Courtesy Union Hall Association.)

WHITTIER: A popular tearoom, ice cream, and soda snack bar in the 1930s, this little building still stands in the shadow of the home of "bigger than life" former Carroll County High Sheriff Jim Welch. (Courtesy Steve Damon.)

TAMWORTH: This building served as a residence upstairs and a store downstairs. It burned c. 1929. Edna Cummings Mason rebuilt and it's the home of her grandson today. Note the white slats of the old wooden bridge to the right which spanned the Swift River in the village of Tamworth. (Courtesy Millie Streeter.)

TAMWORTH: "Mom" Garland's Cash Store (c. 1950s) at the four corners carried just about anything—and if it wasn't in stock she would "order it for you" even, according to some local youth's tale, if it was striped paint. (Courtesy Elva Bickford.)

ALBANY: The White Ledge Store (c. 1930) was destroyed in the 1950s and rebuilt in 1953. Today it is owned by Alexandra Perry and serves as an apartment. (Courtesy G. and R. Morrill.)

PASSACONAWAY: The Russell/Colbath house, located on Kancamagus Highway, was built in 1831–32 by Thomas Russell and his son Amzi. Amzi's daughter Ruth married Thomas Colbath and served as the first postmaster for Passaconaway from 1890 to 1906 in this, her home. In 1891 Thomas left the house on an errand and never returned. For thirty-nine years Ruth faithfully left a lamp in the window to guide him home. Three years after her death, he showed up—an old man—with vague tales of travel afar and then left again. The farm, placed on National Register of Historic Places in 1987, was purchased in 1961 by the U.S. Forest Service and today serves as an information center and a museum of early NH life. (Courtesy Elaine Wales.)

SOUTH TAMWORTH: According to the Old Home Week 1906 booklet, John T.D. Folsom was appointed postmaster on May 11, 1846; either he or his wife (she was a Republican and he was a Democrat) ran the post office for over sixty years. For a few years the post office was in Elizabeth Maddox's house (now Lane's), but it returned to this building until 1959, when Carl Bickford opened the present post office. (Courtesy Elva Bickford.)

SOUTH TAMWORTH: Mrs. Elizabeth Maddox reigns as postmistress in the left front room of her home (now Lane's house) amid her Victorian surroundings. (Courtesy Union Hall Association.)

TAMWORTH: Remick's Grocery—shown here as Pollard's Store (renters)—was eventually reclaimed by Earl and Waddy Remick, who resumed the family business until their deaths in the 1970s. It is a grocery store today owned by Carol and Frank Vernava. (Courtesy Millie Streeter.)

ALBANY: The Hill and Waddell Mill was one of the earliest lumber companies in the Wonalancet area. Edgar Page, son of Moses Page, reminisced in a 1950s interview: "There was a little community called Slab City . . . I think there were 15 or 20 families. There was a company store and a big boarding house . . . They were mostly natives, a few from outside who worked in the woods and some colored men from Nova Scotia and around there . . . It was water operated and there was a canal to get overshot water for the wheel . . ." (Courtesy Elaine Wales.)

CHOCORUA: The Alonzo Nickerson Mill was located on the Chocorua River at the north end of Chocorua Lake. It was originally owned by Phin Tibbetts and was in operation in 1872. Alonzo's son Ezra later managed the mill. They had horizontal wheel, shingle, saw, and threshing operations upstairs with the gristmill on the lower floor. The sawmill was dismantled about 1917 and the machinery went to Rollinsford; the rest went to Theodore Brown, and in 1974 to the Squam Lake Science Center in Holderness. (Courtesy Tamworth Historical Society.)

SOUTH TAMWORTH: South Tamworth Industries making custom millwork—furniture and toys—was started by Farwell Bemis in the 1920s. The building burned in the 1940s. (Courtesy Steve Damon.)

OSSIPEE: The S.J. Thompson and Son Mill was started in the 1870s on the Beech River in the Hackney area. Logs were received in the building at the left; lumber was prepared for construction of houses in the buildings to the right. The mill was sold to J.F. Chevalier in 1916. No sign of the buildings remain today. (Courtesy Ossipee Historical Society.)

CENTER OSSIPEE: John Sanborn built a saw and gristmill on the Beech River in the 1790s. Joseph Buswell owned the mills in 1800, Nathaniel Libby in 1816, and sometime before 1850 it became Smarts Mill. Today the mill still runs, making shutters and blinds, and is known as the Beech River Mill Company on old Route 16. (Courtesy Steve Damon.)

MOULTON'S MILL: The mill site on the Moultonville mill pond was first used by Maylon Clark about 1819 as the location for a small saw and gristmill. In the 1820s Mark, then Simeon, and finally John Moulton enlarged and expanded the plant. After bankruptcy in the panic of 1857, Lorenzo Moulton gained control of the business in 1858 and it became the largest lumber operation in town. (Courtesy Steve Damon.)

WEST OSSIPEE: White's Garage was built in 1910–11 by Virgil White and it became the area's largest Ford garage, as well as the home of the first snowmobile. Phil Dodge of Sandwich bought the business in 1976 and then sold to Battles about 1978. The building burned in 1978 or 1979. It was rebuilt and then went to the Isuzu auto company and now is owned by Johnson Gas. (Courtesy Steve Damon.)

Three
Sun Up to Sun Down

The earliest homes were farms—starting as cabins or simple capes and expanding with ells, barns, outbuildings, and outhouses. Some of the original farms remain today in the Lower Mount Washington Valley.

ALBANY: On the back of this *c.* 1890s picture is inscribed "Mr. Currier." This is believed to be Hi Currier (father of Edwin and grandfather of Roland) at the door of the barn looking out at his pigs. The Currier farm was located within the jurisdiction of three towns: Albany, Sandwich, and Wonalancet (Tamworth). According to Jesse Ambrose, reminiscing in 1957: "Hi Currier used to say he and his wife slept in the same bedroom but she was in Sandwich and he was in Albany." (Courtesy Tamworth Historical Society.)

CHOCORUA: Ridgehaven Farm, a turkey farm managed by Irene Goodson and located across from George Roberts' farm on Page Hill (originally known as Washburn Hill), was an experimental farm owned by Quaker Oats. (Courtesy Tamworth Historical Society.)

WONALANCET: Buzz Read and Wes Taggert on the Fordson tractor mowing at the Read Farm in Wonalancet. (Courtesy Helen Steele.)

ALBANY: The Sumner Hammond family stand in front of their home *c.* 1910. Today the red house at the Pine Knoll campgrounds on old Route 16 is owned by Philip and Diane Martinello. (Courtesy G. and R. Morrill.)

ALBANY: The Ina and Louis Morrill home (see p. 104) on Route 16 is now owned by a grandson, Franklin Kinslow. Previous owners had been John and Sadie King. (Courtesy G. and R. Morrill.)

ALBANY: A Moulton was one of the earliest settlers and farmed on Bald Hill in 1806. The Moulton farm was located on Birch Hill Road near the Samuel Littlefield house. (Courtesy Elaine Wales.)

ALBANY: The George Morrill house (c. 1915) is located on Route 16. Its exact age is unknown but it is quite old. It has handmade nails and clapboards of uniform thickness. The rear of the house was shingled. Jane Brown once owned the building. (Courtesy G. and R. Morrill.)

ALBANY: Stephen Allard built this house in the late 1700s. It was sold to Orlando Allard in 1864, to T.J. Allard in 1867, and to Burgess Kent in 1873. In 1880 David Hurley swapped his farm and $500 for this sightly farm and land. The farm was passed down through the family to Sarah Hurley Tewksbury and then to Alice Tewksbury Cook before finally being sold out of the family at her death in 1981. It has since been torn down. (Courtesy Elaine Wales.)

ALBANY: In 1866 Samuel Littlefield moved with his family to this beautiful site in the Birch Hill/Bald Hill area with Moat Mountain in the background. He was active in the community and served in the state legislature. This farmhouse is now the Darby Field Inn. (Courtesy Elaine Wales.)

ALBANY: The Alexandra Perry house stands next to the former snack bar on Route 16. In the background is the home of George and Ruth Morrill. (Courtesy G. and R. Morrill.)

WATER VILLAGE: This is the Weeks/Beane house, which still stands today on Route 171 near Water Village (see p. 99). (Courtesy Ossipee Historical Society.)

OSSIPEE: This is a glass-plate print of Colby Chamber's home on Moultonville Road. It looks exactly the same today and is owned by the Warren family. (Courtesy Ossipee Historical Society.)

OSSIPEE: Tom and Bessie Brown's home burned *c.* 1915. Violet Brown Sawyer stands by the tree; her brother Clyde is on the step. (Courtesy Beryl Kramer.)

OSSIPEE: Aubrey Moulton's homestead was destroyed by fire *c.* 1915. It had been located to the left of the Ossipee Insurance Agency. (Courtesy Beryl Kramer.)

OSSIPEE: Aubrey Moulton and his family moved into the right side of this duplex after the *c.* 1915 fire that destroyed his home (see above). Judge Reed lived on the left side and his family is seated on the porch. This house burned as well *c.* 1927. (Courtesy Beryl Kramer.)

OSSIPEE: This is a glass-plate print of the Fred Hodge house on Massachusetts Avenue near Chickville Road. According to Mark Winkley, Mrs. Hodge would drive Fred by horse and buggy to work every day at the dowel mill in Center Ossipee on Dore Street and then pick him up at night. The buggy sits in the dooryard to the right. The present owners, the Preston family, have records going back over two hundred years indicating the homestead was handed down through the Hodge family until about twenty years ago. (Courtesy Ossipee Historical Society.)

WHITTIER: In 1794 Walter Bryant III built his home on the banks of the Bearcamp River; it is now used as a woodshed. As the family grew he added a larger room, which was later used as a barn. In 1878 a one-and-a-half-story house (shown here c. 1890s) was built by another Bryant. Ten generations have occupied this house continually; Florence Bryant Smith's grandson, George Smith, lives here today. (Courtesy George Smith.)

SOUTH TAMWORTH: The Pike Perkins homestead (c. 1918) is located on Bunker Hill Road near Bennett's corner. On the porch are sisters Mary Perkins (later Clancy) and Alice Perkins (later Roberts). In a 1950s interview, Elmer Cummings remembered when there was a race track back of the Perkins place. At one time this farm was considered one of the most productive in the area. Today it is the home of the Community School. (Courtesy Union Hall Association.)

TAMWORTH: The "Other Store," owned by Kate Thompson today, is shown when it was the Varney home. It became Woodbine Cottage in the late 1800s and the owners took in summer boarders. Later the Pollards owned it—living in the left end by the river and on the right end offering a variety of merchandise. The Remick brothers bought the building in 1950s and tore down the section with the living quarters—leaving the right section as a department store. (Courtesy Millie Streeter.)

SOUTH TAMWORTH: The Charles J. Ames residence (*c.* 1900) is located on Route 25. Mr. Ames received an academic and commercial college education, taught school eight years, and then became a lumber dealer. The house is now owned by the Stowbridge family. (Courtesy Union Hall Association.)

TAMWORTH: Reverend Franklin Davis (see p. 91) lived in this house on Route 113 when it was the parsonage for the Tamworth Congregational Church from 1875 to 1884. It was later owned by Charlie Remick's parents—Helen Wheeler Remick and Harry Herbert Remick (see p. 88). Today it's owned by Nate Hughes. (Courtesy Millie Streeter.)

TAMWORTH: The Mary and Henry Banks house (*c.* 1900) is in the village at the four corners. Mr. and Mrs. Banks had owned the Banks Hotel (later called the Bearcamp River House) in West Ossipee. Mary Banks is the woman in black on the porch; the woman in white is Ethel Quinby, Barbara Fromm's mother (see p. 92). The house is now broken up into apartments. (Courtesy Barbara Fromm.)

CHOCORUA: The old Perkins house, photographed in 1882, is situated on the now busy corner of Route 16 and 113. It later became Pascoe's store, then Hamel's Real Estate, and today is a mixture of stores and businesses. (Courtesy Tamworth Historical Society.)

TAMWORTH: The Thomas and Hannah Wiggin home is located on the four corners in the village. It is now an apartment house. (Courtesy Tamworth Historical Society.)

TAMWORTH: In 1879 Lucy Jackson Blake (see pp. 64 and 85) bought this farm and 100 acres from Isaiah Cushing. Lucy and her son Harry managed the farm and orchard and also opened a summer boarding house. After Lucy and then Harry died, the house on Gardner Hill Road went to Ned and Rhoda Johnson, later to Christine Johnson Hidden, and today is owned by Tom and Bonnie Herget. (Courtesy Judy Schibanoff.)

TAMWORTH: The Miss Margaret Lincoln Fay house on Route 113 is now owned by her descendants, the Lincoln Robinson family. The house was built c. 1796; the first owner of record was John Clarke of Beverly, Massachusetts, who married Parson Hidden's sister Eunice. (Courtesy Millie Streeter.)

TAMWORTH: The foundation of this long-abandoned farm on Hollow Hill Road is all that remains of the home of Reverend Samuel Kingsbury. He was the father of Josiah Weare Babcock Kingsbury, the grandfather of George Deane Kingsbury, and the great-grandfather of Edward and Aileen Kingsbury. The property is now owned by the Freeman Woodward family. (Courtesy Judy Schibanoff.)

WHITTIER: Walter Evans is standing by his horses in the field opposite his farm—handed down by his grandfather Isaiah Hodson—on old Route 25 in the early 1900s. Ebenezer Dow built what is probably one of the earliest houses in town and became licensed as a taverner. A subsequent owner was the father-in-law of Kate Douglas Wiggin; the Wiggins ran it as a stagecoach stop and inn. The house has deteriorated and the present owner has partially dismantled this once lovely home on the Bearcamp River. (Courtesy Tamworth Historical Society.)

TAMWORTH: Charles Jackson built this farmhouse for his bride in 1824. The homestead was handed down through the family until the 1950s. The barn is long gone. The home is now owned by the Ulitz family. (Courtesy Ulitz Family.)

SOUTH TAMWORTH: This farmhouse has been the home of Perley and Gertrude Ryder since 1952. Previous owners were Pike Perkins, Harvey Moulton, Charles Perkins, and Charles Whiting. (Courtesy Steve Damon.)

CHOCORUA: Originally this farm was occupied by the Salvage family from 1842 until 1869. Professor William James bought the home and 75 acres located on Route 16 in 1886 and it remained in the distinguished James family for almost eighty years. (Courtesy M. and J. Hidden.)

WONALANCET: Clara and Richard Read and friends stand in front of the home which they purchased in 1928 on the Chinook Trail with some of the sled dogs they raised. Hiram Wiggin was the original owner in 1844 followed by Henry and Hannah W. Wiggin and then Thomas and Hannah D. Wiggin. Ira Tilton and his wife came to Locke Falls Cottage and ran the inn in the early 1900s. Today it is the private residence of the Cargills. (Courtesy Nancy Coville.)

WONALANCET: The Mt. Mexico farm was bought in the mid-1950s by James Breasted and it remains in the family today. An ad in the 1906 Old Home Week booklet notes that Fred Bickford is the proprietor. In a 1950s interview Walter Jones mentioned an unusual incident involving Walter Walker and Fred Bickford: "His brother-in-law Fred Bickford on Mt. Mexico Farm froze to death outside his home and Walter brought him down on a hand sled." Roland Currier once said about his grandfather: "The old Mt. Mexico farm was set off. They put a jog in for my grandfather. Grandfather had to go to Albany to vote until then." The insert map on p. 6 shows the jog at the Tamworth/Albany line. (Courtesy Steve Damon.)

Ex-President Clevelands Residence, Tamworth, N. H.

TAMWORTH: President Grover Cleveland's summer home was built around 1830 by James Remick and inherited in turn by John Remick and Francis Remick, who sold it to the President in 1904. An expansion from a small farm to a twenty-room house with nine baths and eleven bedrooms was a necessity to accommodate the hordes of people of all ages, servants aplenty, and much activity. The house was recently sold out of the family. (Courtesy Steve Damon.)

CHOCORUA: This was the summer residence *c.* 1912 of the Honorable J.S. (Sumner) Runnells, born in 1864 to Elder and Huldah Staples Runnells. In a 1950s interview Mrs. Sylvia Bowditch said: "The Runnells house was taken down 1936–1938. It was built by Mr. Peabody of Peabody and Strauss—a prominent architectural firm in Boston." It has been said it was torn down because of a dispute with the town over taxes. (Courtesy Steve Damon.)

Four

Rest for the Weary Traveler

Many homes and farms were turned into boarding houses and inns to handle the ever-increasing crowds of visitors. Summer tourists came for the season and arrived with trunks and even servants. Many of the old lodging places have burned or been torn down but there still remain a few long-standing inns and hotels.

OSSIPEE VILLAGE: The beautiful Carroll Inn is shown here in the late 1800s. To add to its charm, three horse-chestnut trees grew through the floor of the porch, shading the guests. It was located across the street from the courthouse and was considered one of the best hotels in the area. Brackett Wiggin bought the Josiah Poland house, enlarged it, and ran it as a tavern; Thomas Wiggin, his son, succeeded him. The inn burned in 1921 and was not rebuilt. (Courtesy Beryl Kramer.)

CENTER OSSIPEE: The log dining hall of the Indian Mound Camp was located on the present-day Indian Mound Golf Course; the camp extended across the road. (Courtesy Steve Damon.)

OSSIPEE: Jacob Brown built Ossipee's earliest inn and his son John expanded the "Old Brown House" in the 1810s. A commercial hotel, it stood where the present post office is now. Its popularity gradually declined under the ownership of Adam and Moses Brown and it was eventually razed. (Courtesy Beryl Kramer.)

CENTER OSSIPEE: Listed in the business directory as Central House from 1884 to 1924, it became the Center Ossipee Inn in 1925 and served the community until it closed in 1979. (Courtesy Steve Damon.)

WEST OSSIPEE: The Mount Whittier House served as a boarding house in the early 1900s. It is now privately owned by the McGlinchey family. (Courtesy Steve Damon.)

WEST OSSIPEE: Hotels and inns are strung along the Bearcamp River. The most famous was the Bearcamp River House (formerly the Ames Tavern and then Banks Hotel), a favorite vacation destination for poet John Greenleaf Whittier. The hotel burned *c.* 1880 and was never rebuilt. (Courtesy Charles Remick.)

WONALANCET: John Sanborn first operated Edgehill Inn in the early part of the century. His grandfather had cleared the land and built a one-and-a-half-story house. It's now the private residence of Reverend and Mrs. James Johnson. (Courtesy Tamworth Historical Society.)

TAMWORTH: Sadie Stevens owned The Maples on Route 113 in the mid-1920s when Gladys Corbett Evans boarded here as a young teacher. Before that an ad in the 1906 Old Home Week booklet indicated that C.P. Johnson was the proprietor and that it was: ". . . open from June 1st to November 1st . . . Excellent table—Large airy rooms—Broad piazzas from which magnificent views of the mountains can be had . . ." It is now a private residence. (Courtesy Charles Remick.)

TAMWORTH: Frank (his trusty Model T sits in the dooryard) and Florentine Carle ran the Whittier Lodge as a boarding house in the 1930s; later Ethel and Everett Berry owned it and served dinner to the Barnstormers in the summer. It is now privately owned by Lorraine and Clifford Streeter. (Courtesy Millie Streeter.)

TAMWORTH: The former Parson Hidden farm, built in the late 1700s or early 1800s, became the Mountain Park Cottage in the late 1800s and offered room and board in the summers. The house is long gone but in 1955 a home was built over the old foundation by Mrs. Myrick Crane. (Courtesy Steve Damon.)

TAMWORTH: Idlewilde was one of the cottages built by George Deane Kingsbury early in the twentieth century for summer visitors. The cottages are still in the hands of his descendants at the corner of Gardner Hill Road and Route 113-A (see p. 86). (Courtesy Judy Schibanoff.)

TAMWORTH: Three Trees was another boarding house next to The Maples on Route 113 and was run by Theresa Sampson. It is now a private residence. (Courtesy Cook Memorial Library.)

WONALANCET: Caleb Brown built this farm in 1814 and it was handed down through his family. Kate Sleeper Walden bought the homestead in 1890 and converted it into an inn, The Wonalancet Farm, and ran it until 1930. Within a year of its opening, *Sweetser's Guide to the White Mountains* was recommending the inn with its beautiful mountain views, meadows, brooks, library, and chapel. It is now the home of Katherine Ainsworth Semmes. (Courtesy Steve Damon.)

TAMWORTH: Lucy Blake sits on the steps with her guests at Sunset Cottage, located on Gardner Hill Road (see pp. 51 and 85). She opened her farmhouse to summer boarders to supplement her income sometime in the 1880s. In 1890 Kate Sleeper Walden was a guest; she liked it so much she searched the area for a suitable place, and found and purchased what became The Wonalancet Farm (see previous page). (Courtesy Judy Schibanoff.)

TAMWORTH: Willow Inn was supposedly built by Joseph Gilman in the early 1800s. It became the Willow Inn in the 1880s under the management of George Ed Gilman. In 1882 the register included some quite exotic guests: forty-four members of the Van Amburgh Menagerie, ventriloquists, comic vocalists, baseball players, cornet band members, glass blowers, and more! There was much excitement in Tamworth in the 1880s! Today the building serves a more mundane purpose, housing the town offices; the annex is the home of the Tamworth Community Nurse Association. (Courtesy Steve Damon.)

CHOCORUA: In 1870 John Henry Nickerson and his wife Clarinda were among the first people to open their home to summer boarders. An ad in the 1906 Old Home booklet states: ". . . Chocorua Hotel and Cottages . . . beautifully situated, looking directly across Chocorua Lake, upon Mt. Chocorua and other mountains of the Sandwich Range . . . M.E. Robertson . . . Manager." In a 1922 booklet A.B. Atwood is listed as Manager. The building was torn down in the mid-1940s. (Courtesy Elva Bickford.)

TAMWORTH: In the early 1900s dances were held on the second floor of the big barn at Ansel Cummings' Waukaneto House until a c. 1909 fire destroyed the buildings. Ansel was the grandfather of Theresa Mason Chase and Joyce Mason Jones. (Courtesy Charles Remick.)

CHOCORUA: The Old Home booklet of 1906 indicates John S. Hayford was proprietor of Hayfords in the Field. L.D. Hayford was the owner in 1922, when an advertisement in the Tamworth Winter Carnival booklet mentioned the added enticement of "furnace heat." Since the 1960s Fred and Ramona Stafford have owned the lovely inn, now appropriately called Stafford's-in-the-Field. (Courtesy Steve Damon.)

CHOCORUA: The Chocorua View House is shown *c.* 1930s with Mr. and Mrs. Benjamin Ward as hosts. Before the Wards, it was owned by the Walkers; after the Wards came the Hoch family; and today it is a thriving bed and breakfast on busy Route 16. (Courtesy Steve Damon.)

TAMWORTH: This building was opened as the Wiggin House in the late 1880s with Arthur "El" Wiggin as proprietor. He added wings to each end of the house and introduced "Electric annunciator and modern improvements," but evidently over-extended himself and had to sell. It continued as the popular Tamworth Inn under various owners through the years and today is in the capable hands of the Bender family. (Courtesy Tamworth Historical Society.)

CHOCORUA: The origins of this home are unknown but Phineas Tibbetts bought the place in 1869. He farmed and ran a mill on Chocorua River (see p. 36). Later Maud M. and G. Wallace Tibbetts managed the homestead as Ramblers Rest Inn on Route 16. Note the poignant message on the postcard from Wallace about his childhood home. In 1965 the last owners, the Ralph Raabes, opened Slop Chest, selling fine antiques. (Courtesy Ralph Raabe.)

Ferncroft, Wonalancet, N. H.

ALBANY: Ferncroft Inn (formerly the home of the Currier brothers) was established by Mr. and Mrs. Elliot Fisher in 1908. Close to many hiking trails, it attracted skilled climbers from all over. The owners added cabins and separate dining quarters and could accommodate over one hundred guests, including many professional and university families. It burned in 1966. (Courtesy Steve Damon.)

ALBANY: The Red Eagle Boarding House was built in the late 1700s and was used as a home, grain store, and inn. Located in the Canada Street area, it burned in 1955. Anson P. Irish, the owner, is pictured on the right; his wife, Nellie Irish, is second from the left. (Courtesy G. and R. Morrill.)

ALBANY: This is the actual fire on June 9, 1940, of the Clement Inn. Also called the Piper House and Wings Tavern, the inn was located on Route 16 in Albany. A 1909 leaflet sent to prospective guests lists E.R. Robertson as manager, the railway station as Madison (a stage met all trains), and the post office address as Pequaket. (Courtesy Elaine Wales.)

PASSACONAWAY: Thomas Shackford built this farm, and his son James later ran it as a year-round inn. President Cleveland and his young wife stayed here at times. In 1907 Alfred Povall bought the place and he and his son ran the inn as the Passaconaway House. The buildings burned in 1916. (Courtesy Elaine Wales.)

ALBANY: Jim Liberty sold his Chocorua Mountain Road and Halfway House to David Knowles of Silver Lake. David built the Chocorua Peak House in either 1884 or 1891 and offered food and lodging to all who climbed to the summit for its fabulous view. Although the structure was anchored to the ledges with chains and had withstood storms of great strength, on an autumn night in 1915 gales tore the building from its moorings and scattered it over the mountainside. It was never rebuilt. (Courtesy G. and R. Morrill.)

Five
For the Good Times

The need to entertain the visitors created further industry. Entertainment was, and still is, one of the valley's greatest promotions, and includes theater, music, the arts, puppetry, square dancing, skiing, snowshoeing, skating, snowmobiling, dog sledding, ice fishing, stream and lake fishing, and much more.

SOUTH TAMWORTH: Union Hall (c. 1900) was built in 1894 and was the center of social activities. Note the watering trough on the left and E.L. Mason's Socony sign on the right. Traveling shows, local plays, box suppers, church donations, promenades, and more were held here. Dancing was prohibited as being unsuitable for church-going people; so promenades were substituted (see p. 79). Hooker Moody once explained: ". . . a promenade was just a march . . . We'd go round and go up the center and then ladies go one way and men the other . . . Then they come up the center, woman would cross ahead of the man . . . Then they'd group 4 abreast and then 8 abreast." Times changed and Union Hall eventually voted to allow dancing. (Courtesy Steve Damon.)

SOUTH TAMWORTH: Mason Hall was the setting for movies, dances, and general fun in the 1920s and 1930s. (Courtesy Steve Damon.)

TAMWORTH: Tamworth Gardens (c. 1931) was used for everything—basketball, boxing, and even as a stage for plays; *Ghost Train*, a long enduring favorite, was first done here in 1931. The Barnstormers still use the building for rehearsals. (Courtesy Francis Cleveland.)

PINELAND. CENTER OSSIPEE. N. H.

CENTER OSSIPEE: Pineland Center—built in 1929—was the town hall, movie theater, dance hall, and in the 1930s even served as a church until the Catholic church was constructed. The building is now used as Ossipee's Town Hall. (Courtesy Steve Damon.)

OSSIPEE: Members of the Ossipee Lake Grange pose after their minstrel show. (Courtesy Ossipee Historical Society.)

73

OSSIPEE LAKE: Ray Stillings is racing his sulky on Ossipee Lake on February 22, 1925. Horse racing on ice was a favorite winter sport in all three towns. (Courtesy Ossipee Historical Society.)

ALBANY: Snowmobiling was a new and exciting winter sport in the 1940s. The trailers were the offices for snowmobile races. Mt. Chocorua is at the right in the background. (Courtesy G. and R. Morrill.)

ALBANY: The crew who ran the snowmobile races stand around with a few of the racers in the field across from Elizabeth Coleman. A young Willard Croto is on the right. (Courtesy G. and R. Morrill.)

ALBANY: Girls from Pine Knoll Camp hiking Mt. Chocorua in the 1920s stop for a rest at the "shelter" which was located on the ledges on the back side of the mountain. The building, now long gone, was used as sleeping quarters by the fire wardens. (Courtesy G. and R. Morrill.)

TAMWORTH: This corn husking party was held at Harry Damon's barn on Cleveland Hill Road in 1939. From front to back are: (left) Marian Anderson, Elsie Gilman, Hilda Johnson (Ross), Ken Knowlton, Steve Damon, Everett Henderson, Ida Mahoney, Harry Henderson, and Almon and Gladys Evans; (right) Perley Grace, Patricia Damon, Howard Grace, and other friends. (Courtesy Cook Memorial Library.)

TAMWORTH: A Tamworth Outing Club square dance was held one Christmas at Huckins Barn on Great Hill Road. The barn was the scene of many dances with "Hidden's Orchestra" (Helen Hidden is at the piano) until the building burned in the 1950s. (Courtesy Elva Bickford.)

SOUTH TAMWORTH: At the top of "Hidden Hill" in February 1916 are Marjorie T. Gregg (on the right), niece Alice Bemis Thompson (left), nephew Alan (behind Alice), and niece Faith (in the distance). (Courtesy Kate Thompson.)

TAMWORTH: A women's snowshoe race was held at the 1922 Tamworth Winter Carnival in Clough's field. The intrepid racers are Alice Alley, Edna Alley, Leona Bodge, Claire Moody, Eunice Hidden, Margaret Steele, and Elizabeth Hidden. Alice's husband Dan is acting as starter. (Courtesy Millie Streeter.)

TAMWORTH: The Tamworth Tigers was the name of the town baseball team; in the 1920s they were thought to be of semi-professional caliber. From left to right are: (front row) Everett Bunker, Lincoln Steele, and Wadsworth (Waddy) Remick; (back row) Aldo Stearns, Roland Currier, Dana Steele, Ned Johnson, Frank Bunker, and Earle Remick. (Courtesy Tamworth Historical Society.)

TAMWORTH: Unidentified skiers are being pulled by rope tow up Page Hill sometime in the 1940s. The Civilian Conservation Corps had done the preliminary clearing on Page Hill and the Tamworth Outing Club (Ned Behr, Buzz Read, and Lincoln Steele) had done the rest to make this one of the first ski tows in the area. (Courtesy Helen Steele.)

78

CHOCORUA: Included in this photograph of a Women's Club Masquerade Party at Runnells Hall in the 1940s are Vickie Brett, Priscilla Brown, George Underhill, Natalie Hobbs, Harold Wiggin, Louise Hobbs, Manley Brett, Marian Corbett, Lawrence Brett, Stella Hobbs, Walter Doe, Evelyn Doe, and Waino Autio. This scene portrays a typical promenade (see p. 71). (Courtesy Cook Memorial Library.)

CHOCORUA: This Women's Club Christmas party took place at the old Runnells Hall. At the piano is Helen Hidden, Kennett Hunt is on drums, Fred Moore is thought to be on the sax, and Earl Jones is at the trumpet. The young man against wall is Clifford "Chummy" Streeter, and the boy in front on the left is David Remick. (Courtesy J. and M. Hidden.)

TAMWORTH: The actors and crew pose in front of the vehicle used by the Barnstormers in the mid-1930s. Included in the picture are Ed Goodnow, James Sever, Hal Meyer, Francis Cleveland, Helen Ray, Clara Butler, Stephen Green, Phil Bourneuf, Linda Collins, Brenda Dahlin, and Felice Leeds. The driver is George Quimby. (Courtesy Francis Cleveland.)

TAMWORTH: These horseback riders in the 1931 Tamworth Pageant are, from left to right: Ralph Taylor (Sandwich), Marian Spaulding, Evelyn Spaulding Wallace, and Paul Taylor (Sandwich). (Courtesy Millie Streeter.)

WHITTIER: George Bryant, Lizzie Bryant, and Edith Provost (the others are unknown) are boating on the Bearcamp River around 1904. Mt. Whittier is in the background. (Courtesy George Smith.)

TAMWORTH: Gertrude Blackey competes in the "rolling pin throw" on Old Home Day in 1929. The gentleman on her left is Samuel Hidden, followed by Charlie Hammond, Richard Clapp, and Kenneth Knowlton. To the rear of Kenneth is Jack Leach; after Kenneth are Richard Stearns, Stanley Trask, and to his rear, Fred Steele. (Courtesy Tamworth Historical Society.)

TAMWORTH: This wonderful picture was, of course, taken at Ordination Rock, but the date and the names of the tennis players are unknown. Mary Trask, Barnstormers' expert costumer, places it at around the turn of the century. She also noted that both young men have wide belts with snake buckles—perhaps a clue to a college or club? (Courtesy Tamworth Historical Society.)

WONALANCET: Arthur T. Walden, driving his sled dog team on a well-known trail, learned his skills dog freighting in Alaska. In Wonalancet he raised and trained dogs and brought sled dog racing to the area. He was with Admiral Byrd on Byrd's first expedition to the Antarctic (see p. 126). (Courtesy Tamworth Historical Society.)

Six
The Conquerors

The faces in faded photographs taken in the 1800s and early 1900s are often stern, strong, and somber, showing the strength of character and independence so indicative of our early settlers. We also see the evidence of unending labor, harsh weather, and, occasionally, the lack of good dentists.

TAMWORTH: The crew at the Tamworth Inn lined up for this photograph in the late 1880s. From left to right are: (front row) Henry Robinson, Bartlett Durgin, El Wiggin (owner), and Charles Cram; (back row) George "Jigger" Hatch, Larkin Weed, Colonel Dow, Ambrose Sanger (the chef who had a wooden leg), Thorne Whitten, William Blaisdell, Ed Currier, and John Robinson (waiter). (Courtesy Tamworth Historical Society.)

SOUTH TAMWORTH: Honorable Larkin D. Mason (1811–1903) was one of the most highly regarded citizens of Tamworth. He was a member of the New Hampshire Senate and House, a probate judge, and, during the Civil War, was a military agent who gained eminent respect and ended the war with the rank of Colonel. Born and bred in South Tamworth, he was active in the Methodist Church, the local school district, and was a speaker of great eloquence and wit. (Courtesy Tamworth Historical Society.)

CHOCORUA: Reverend John Runnells (1817–1887), for whom Runnells Hall is named, is shown here in the 1880s with his wife, Huldah Staples (1819–1906). Elder Runnells was the minister in the Chocorua Baptist Church (see p. 21) from 1852 until his death. Alice James, his grandchild and the wife of William James, said in a mid-1950s interview: "There seems to be but one opinion of my grandfather . . . he was beloved by all." (Courtesy Tamworth Historical Society.)

TAMWORTH: Elizabeth Storey Deane Jackson from Gilmanton married Charles Jackson of Tamworth in 1824 and moved into the farmhouse he had built for her (see p. 53). She died in 1892. Some of the descendants of her eleven children still summer on nearby Kingsbury property. (Courtesy Judy Schibanoff.)

TAMWORTH: Lucy Jackson Blake, born in 1834, is shown here at some point shortly before the Civil War. She kept diaries of most of her adult years—giving us a true picture of life in Tamworth during the last half of the nineteenth century. She taught school in her early years, married, had one son, and was widowed when her husband died in the Civil War. In 1879 she bought Isaiah Cushing's farm of 100 acres and soon after opened one of the early boarding houses (see pp. 51 and 64). (Courtesy Judy Schibanoff.)

TAMWORTH: Lucy Deane Page (1809–1893) was the sister of Elizabeth Deane Jackson (see p. 85), the wife of Jabez Page, and the ancestress of Horace Page, Howard Page, Ruth Page Marshall, Millie Marshall Streeter, Laurie Marshall Nixon, et al. Lucy was known for her prodigious spinning and weaving. Her father, Benjamin Deane, fought in the Battle of Lexington. (Courtesy Judy Schibanoff.)

TAMWORTH: George Deane Kingsbury (c. 1900) was the son of Mary Jackson and Josiah Kingsbury. He bought land from Joe Bodge near the Jackson farm, next to Lucy Blake's Sunset Cottage, and built summer cottages in among the trees. His cottages remain today in the family (see p. 62). (Courtesy Judy Schibanoff.)

TAMWORTH: John Deering Hidden (1829–1902) was a well-known businessman and farmer and owner of the Hartford Insurance Company's first agency in the area. His diary says he spent long weeks traveling by horse and buggy on country roads taking care of insurance business and selling subscriptions to the *Carroll County History* (1889). He was a grandson of Parson Samuel Hidden. (Courtesy J. and M. Hidden.)

TAMWORTH: Before washing machines the cool waters of the Swift River and a bar of homemade soap often served the purpose. On the left in this *c.* 1912 photograph is Helen Basset Hidden (1893–1964) and on the right is her mother-in-law, Elizabeth Bellows Hidden (1867–1942). Helen Hidden was librarian at Cook Memorial Library from 1930 until her death. (Courtesy J. and M. Hidden.)

TAMWORTH: Former President Grover Cleveland doing some yard work at his Tamworth home. His son Francis said "he probably was digging worms. I never knew him to do any work." Fishing was his favorite above all activities. In the background, his sons Richard (age 10) and Francis (age 4) would go on to become well known in their own right. (Courtesy Francis Cleveland.)

TAMWORTH: Helen Wheeler Remick and Harry Herbert Remick (Charlie Remick's parents) are on the top of Page Hill around the turn of the century. The charming couple undoubtedly climbed the hill in this attire—hats and all! (Courtesy Charles Remick.)

SOUTH TAMWORTH: Hattie Green (1855–1928), born in Madison to Ansel and Forest Green, lived her adult life on Mountain Road in South Tamworth. She married George Moody and had a son, Almon, who became a well-known photographer in Bristol. She was married a second time to Charles Clough. Admired by many, her death brought grief to the community. She is buried in Riverside Cemetery. (Courtesy Tamworth Historical Society.)

TAMWORTH: Cora Larabee (1865–1955) is pictured with her father Hiram Mason (1843–1940). Cora is Richard Stearn's grandmother and Tee Chase and Joyce Jones' great aunt; Hi Mason is their great-grandfather. Hi Mason and his son Ernest built President Cleveland's Memorial Wall (see p. 25). (Courtesy Tamworth Historical Society.)

TAMWORTH: The faces of friends and classmates are captured in this c. 1910 photograph. From left to right are: (front row) Edna Cummings Mason, Agnes Page Pascoe, Eleanor Alley, Serena Remick, and Christina Cole; (back row) Roland Currier, Aldo Stearns, Edson Alley, Harold Trask, and Edna Alley. (Courtesy Tamworth Historical Society.)

SOUTH TAMWORTH: A typical Saturday night c. 1915 gathering at the Maddox porch included, from left to right, Emma Mason, Gertrude Downs, Elizabeth Maddox, Leafy Mason (the sister of Gertrude and wife of Ernest), and Clara Mason (the wife of Harry Mason, who was a selectman for many years). (Courtesy Union Hall Association.)

TAMWORTH: Reverend Franklin Davis served the Tamworth Congregational Church from 1875 to about 1890. He married many Tamworth couples including Harry Lincoln Smith and Florence Bryant of Whittier (parents of Marian Smith). During his pastorate he lived in the parsonage (see p. 49), now Nate Hughes' home. (Courtesy George Smith.)

TAMWORTH: Dr. James Bassett graduated from Bowdoin College following his marriage to Fannie Althea Tilton, his second marriage. On June 27, 1894, Helen J. Bassett was born. The doctor died when Helen was three years old. (Courtesy J. and M. Hidden.)

TAMWORTH: Lucy Hodge Cook (*c.* 1920s) was the wife of Clint Cook and the daughter-in-law of Charles and Susan Cook. Lucy was the first librarian at the Cook Memorial Library (built in memory of her father-in-law), serving from 1892 to 1929. She was also a Sunday school teacher and the first woman in the village to sell bread and homemade ice cream. (Courtesy Tamworth Historical Society.)

TAMWORTH: Ethel E. Quinby (*c.* 1915) was born in North Sandwich in 1887. When she was eleven her father died, and she then lived with her grandmother, Mary Banks, in the village of Tamworth. She married William Willey and their daughter, artist Barbara Willey Fromm, lives in Tamworth today. (Courtesy Barbara Fromm.)

WHITTIER: Marian Edith Smith and her mother, Florence Bryant Smith, of Bryant Farm, are shown here c. 1909. (Courtesy George Smith.)

WONALANCET: The first wedding in the Wonalancet Union Chapel (see p. 22) was the marriage of Richard Read and Clara Enebuske, pictured here with their respective mothers as well as the ever present dog on September 17, 1927. (Courtesy Nancy Coville.)

TAMWORTH: Frank Evans (1862–1948) stands with his wife, Idella Clough (1872–1942), and his grandson, Lyle Grant, in the late 1920s or 1930s. Originally from Moultonboro, Frank had a very successful meat business in Tamworth before building a lumber mill in 1910 on the banks of the Swift River opposite the site of the home he would build in 1914. The mill is gone but the house stands today on the Chinook Trail, having been converted to an apartment building. (Courtesy Tamworth Historical Society.)

TAMWORTH: Fred Remick and Herb Piper were caught in a photograph by Francis Cleveland as they walked through the village. Fred's son was Dexter and his grandson is David of Great Hill Road. Fred and Winnie Remick lived in the Harkness house. Herb Piper lived in the house on the village side of the post office on Route 113 (now the Collier house). Steve Damon remembers Herb with smokepot in hand, covered in protective netting, searching out honey from the wild bees. (Courtesy Francis Cleveland.)

TAMWORTH: Alice and Francis Cleveland (the founders of Barnstormers) pose with two of their long line of beloved terriers. (Courtesy Francis Cleveland.)

TAMWORTH: Charles Wiggin, also caught by Francis Cleveland's camera, served many years on the Tamworth School Board and was highly respected, even feared (however unnecessarily), when he came to inspect the school. His daughter, Estella White, served as registrar of probate in Ossipee for many years. Her son, Richard White, owned and operated White's Funeral Parlor in Conway before his retirement. (Courtesy Francis Cleveland.)

TAMWORTH: Roland Currier (born in 1900) and Hazle Evans Currier (born in 1899) stand in front of Millcrest, the Evans family homestead on Route 113A in the 1930s. Hazle was the daughter of Frank and Dell Evans (see p. 94) and Roland was the son of Edwin Currier, who carried the mail by horse and auto for thirty years and transported summer visitors from West Ossipee station to the various inns and boarding houses. Hi Currier of Wonalancet (see p. 39) was his grandfather. (Courtesy Tamworth Historical Society.)

CHOCORUA: The dam at the foot of Chocorua Lake was put in by Almon Evans (on the right). On the left is Earl Remick, who was selectman at the time. (Courtesy Lorraine Streeter.)

SOUTH TAMWORTH: Elva Floyd
Bickford is held by her great-
grandmother, Sophronia Mason,
in 1914 in front of the latter's home
in Whiteface. (Courtesy
Elva Bickford.)

MOULTONVILLE: This glass-plate
photograph is a self-portrait of Mr. and Mrs.
Herbert White. He was a commercial
photographer whose home was in
Moultonville—his studio was in back of the
store owned by G.L. and C.A. White.
(Courtesy Ossipee Historical Society.)

CENTER OSSIPEE: This glass-plate photograph by H.E. White shows Lucian Nichols in his best attire. Mr. Nichols lived on Moultonville Road and served as a blacksmith during the early 1900s. (Courtesy Ossipee Historical Society.)

OSSIPEE: Cary Wilkins was the first black man in Ossipee. During the Civil War he had been Colonel Quarles' valet and he accompanied the Colonel home to Ossipee at the end of the war. He married, had a family, and became a farmer at his Walker Hill Road home in Ossipee village. The young man on his right is unidentified. (Courtesy Beryl Kramer.)

OSSIPEE: Edmund Brown (1864–1954), the grandson of Adam Taft Brown, grew up in the Hackney area of Ossipee. He worked in civil engineering in Boston and New York and retired to Ossipee. He is shown here addressing the town meeting of March 11, 1914, at the Ossipee YMCA building (burned) near Ossipee Railroad Station. (Courtesy Ossipee Historical Society.)

WATER VILLAGE: Bertha Hersey Beane and Eloise Beane of Water Village were photographed in 1904. Bertha Beane (1878–1969), the daughter of Mary Ellen Weeks and Peter Hersey and the grandchild of Levi and Hepzibah Weeks, married George Beane (1878–1912), the son of Ira and Luella Beane. After George's death, Bertha married James Ricker (1867–1954). Edith Eloise Beane never married but left a heritage to Ossipee in an unpublished history of Water Village. (Courtesy Ossipee Historical Society.)

CHICKVILLE: Alva Dore married Hannah Hanson (see below) and was the father of Ida Dore Bean (1867–1919). He died in 1900 at the age of seventy-seven and is buried in the Chickville Cemetery. (Courtesy Ossipee Historical Society.)

CHICKVILLE: Hannah Hanson Dore, the mother of Ida Bean and the wife of Alva Dore (above), died in 1908 at age eighty-one. She is buried in Chickville Cemetery. (Courtesy Ossipee Historical Society.)

OSSIPEE: Jonathan Dore, husband of Mary, died at age eighty in 1891 and is buried in Chickville Cemetery. He was active in the Freewill Baptist Church in Chickville during his lifetime. (Courtesy Ossipee Historical Society.)

OSSIPEE: This lovely photo portrait is of Charlotte Grant Hodsdon, daughter of Dr. Nathaniel Grant and wife of Arthur Hodsdon, whose home is now the Hitching Post Inn. Her descendants gave Grant Hall to the Ossipee Historical Society in 1923 for use as a museum. (Courtesy Ossipee Historical Society.)

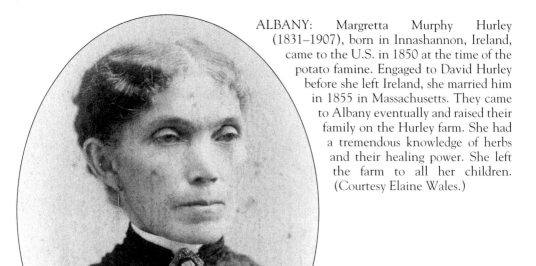

ALBANY: Margretta Murphy Hurley (1831–1907), born in Innashannon, Ireland, came to the U.S. in 1850 at the time of the potato famine. Engaged to David Hurley before she left Ireland, she married him in 1855 in Massachusetts. They came to Albany eventually and raised their family on the Hurley farm. She had a tremendous knowledge of herbs and their healing power. She left the farm to all her children. (Courtesy Elaine Wales.)

ALBANY: David Hurley (1829–1905) followed his fiancee to the U.S. about 1853 and they were married in 1855. He served in the Civil War, and was active in the community, serving as tax collector, town clerk, land agent, selectman, and road agent. He loved his land and built a 50-foot tower so all could see the countryside. (Courtesy Elaine Wales.)

ALBANY: Sarah Hurley Tewksbury (1857–1924) married James Tewksbury of Sandwich in 1877 and they had three children. Upon her mother's death, the Hurley farm became her home again. (Courtesy Elaine Wales.)

ALBANY: Alice Tewksbury Cook, the daughter of Sarah Hurley and James Tewksbury and the sister of Wes Tewksbury, married Frank Cook. She eventually inherited the Hurley farm (see p. 43) upon her mother's death. Upon her own death, the farm was sold out of the family and eventually was torn down. (Courtesy Elaine Wales.)

ALBANY: Irene Hammond, born in Tamworth in 1850, was George Morrill's great aunt. She married George Lansil (1849–1886) and had two children: a daughter, Beulah, who died in infancy, and a son, Arthur (1882–1945). Irene married a Bickford after her husband's death but was buried beside her first husband, George Lansil, in Chocorua Cemetery in 1935. (Courtesy G. and R. Morrill.)

ALBANY: Louis and Ina Morrill pose with sons George and Clyde. It was Ina who first noticed that the Peak House had been blown off Mt. Chocorua in 1915. Louis Morrill came from Nashua and married Ina in 1910. Ina served for over thirty years as tax collector/town clerk. (Courtesy G. and R. Morrill.)

ALBANY: Augusta Bernard Perry (1891–1979) was the daughter of Margretta Hurley and Peter Bernard. Her father managed the farm for Kate Sleeper Walden in Wonalancet. Arthur Walden's tales of Alaska influenced her father's move to Alaska. He was lost in the Arctic in 1916. Augusta married Alpheus Perry in 1916, and became much involved in community affairs: she started the Civic Group, initiated the Lora Johnson Pierce Scholarship Fund, was the chairman of the Albany Bicentennial Committee in 1976, and was a published writer of local history and poetry. She and her husband opened the Golden Age Shop in 1955 and it is still operating today. (Courtesy Elaine Wales.)

ALBANY: Irma and Archie Nickerson lived on the original Samuel Drake farm of 150 acres (Crotos now own the site). Irma taught in different schools for over fifty years. Archie Nickerson served in the legislature in 1925–26. (Courtesy G. and R. Morrill.)

ALBANY: Nathan Brown is thought to be a descendant of one of the earliest Albany settlers—a Nathan Brown also—who was granted 50 acres of land in 1791. The later Nathan Brown was a hoop maker by trade and lived in a log cabin on Blue Mountain. According to William James of Tamworth, Nathan was "a thorough craftsman in wood and stone . . . loved to tell impossible stories." Nathan was born in Albany in 1828 and died in 1915. (Courtesy G. and R. Morrill.)

ALBANY: Jigger Johnson of the Forest Service (in the hat) and a fellow crewman are camped near the summit of Mt. Chocorua. (Courtesy of G. and R. Morrill.)

Seven

Peace in the Valley

The reason for the popularity of the Lower Mount Washington Valley as a vacation destination is due, of course, to our incomparable vistas of lakes, rivers, and mountains, and to our charming villages and our welcoming citizens. "Y'all come to see us when you can."

ALBANY: "Winkley's Gate" marked the end of the road and the entrance to the last house in the intervale. Hobart Winkley married Daisy Hidden, daughter of William Hidden (1837–1924), and this was the entrance to Winkley's summer home. Lena Ford Smith said the house was originally built for Bradbury Jewell's Edgerly mother-in-law. According to Melvin Kimball, "before Winkley owned the furthest house up there, it belonged to Sanford Gilman." The gate—or more likely its replacement—still guards the end of the road; the Ian Cooke family are the present owners. (Courtesy Steve Damon.)

ALBANY: The Chocorua Peak House is centered in this beautiful photograph taken sometime before 1915 from the top of Mt. Chocorua (see p. 70). (Courtesy G. and R. Morrill.)

ALBANY: An unusual view of "The Cow," a boulder on Mt. Chocorua from which Chief Chocorua may have jumped after imposing a curse on Albany, as told in the famous Chocorua legend. (Courtesy G. and R. Morrill.)

ALBANY: The government lookout station on Mt. Chocorua is shown here in 1914. Sam Metcalf, who was in charge of the station, is in the center. (Courtesy Steve Damon.)

ALBANY: Irma Morrill and Dorothea Moore were photographed c. 1920 standing by the side of the dirt road (now Route 16) with the Morrill house in the background. (Courtesy G. and R. Morrill.)

ALBANY: Albany's only covered bridge, located in the Passaconaway area, was built by Amzi Russell in 1857 and is still standing today. (Courtesy G. and R. Morrill.)

CENTER OSSIPEE: The railroad station with its gingerbread trim is at the right in this 1911 scene of Main Street. (Courtesy Steve Damon.)

OSSIPEE CORNER: The corner of Asbury Moulton's home is on the left. Buildings for undertaking equipment, the Carroll Inn, and a delivery stable are at the rear. (Courtesy Beryl Kramer.)

OSSIPEE CORNER: Moulton's store is at the center of this image with the Gile home at the left. (Courtesy Beryl Kramer.)

WEST OSSIPEE: The square is shown with the "new" post office in the distance. (Courtesy Steve Damon.)

OSSIPEE: A neighborhood called "The Bluffs" is shown in this picture of Ossipee Lake. (Courtesy Steve Damon.)

OSSIPEE: The caption on this postcard says "Road to Duncan Lake" (now Route 28). The Flag Gate farm is on the left and the Sias farm is in the background; both buildings are still in place today. (Courtesy Beryl Kramer.)

Center Ossipee, N. H.

CENTER OSSIPEE: The First Congregational Church is at the right. The Hitching Post Inn is at the center; the inn was Dr. Nathaniel Grant's home from 1840 to 1880 and was the home of Levi Perkins before that (1825). (Courtesy Steve Damon.)

WEST OSSIPEE: The Bearcamp Covered Bridge was built by Jacob Berry in 1870 to replace successive open bridges that were washed away. It was on the main route north until the rerouting of Route 16. In 1983 Graton Associates rebuilt the deteriorating bridge but eventually it had to be closed to vehicular traffic. (Courtesy Steve Damon.)

SOUTH TAMWORTH: Horse and buggies trot along on old Main Street where Mason Hill Road crosses, c. 1893. The old blacksmith shop is in the background. Union Hall would be built at the corner on the left in the next year. (Courtesy Union Hall Association.)

TAMWORTH: This image, probably taken in the 1880s or '90s, shows the early wooden bridge that took you over the Swift River and into the village. On the right is the store and upstairs residence (see p. 32) owned by the Cummings family before the fire. (Courtesy Elva Bickford.)

TAMWORTH: In the village looking west we see the Cook Memorial Library on the left with Colonel Dow's home beyond it and then the Tamworth Inn. On the right the Congregational church can be seen with the Currier house—now the Williams place—beyond. (Courtesy Millie Streeter.)

TAMWORTH: Looking east into the village c. 1916, during the days of the horse and buggy, we see Remick's store on the right. Note the extension of the building on the left and the old iron bridge in the background. It had replaced the wooden one on p. 115. (Courtesy Steve Damon.)

TAMWORTH: Across the old mill pond in the village is the home now owned by George and Laura Hubbard—once the Amsah Davis place. In a 1970s interview Perley Grace expressed his feelings about the pond: "I wish they'd put in a new one now—be the biggest improvement in Tamworth. There t'was about 2 acres there we used to go skating on and go swimming there. I was thinkin' if somebody with money would buy that up and make a nice pond there, it would be a big help for the town." (Courtesy Millie Streeter.)

TAMWORTH: This *c.* 1908 view is looking east into the village. The Forrest Ayer home, now owned by Barbara Lloyd and considered the oldest house in Tamworth, is on the left. (Courtesy Tamworth Historical Society.)

TAMWORTH: The Gallagher house on Page Hill is in the center of this photograph with Hayfords in the Field (now Stafford's-in-the-Field) in the distance over the barn. In 1950 Geraldine Bliss Taylor recalled: "Charles Page, son of John McLeary Page, married Mariah Ham. He was in the legislature and he owned the Caroline Gallagher house. It had the first wall paper in this section. That would be my great great grandfather." Elizabeth Allen bought the homestead in 1891, and upon her death the property went to her heirs, the Steele family. They in turn sold it to William and Caroline Gallagher in 1920 and it remains in the Gallagher family today. (Courtesy Tamworth Historical Society.)

CHOCORUA: This photograph of Chocorua village and Chocorua Mountain was taken from Weeks Hill. (Courtesy Steve Damon.)

CHOCORUA: Looking west toward the Chocorua River c. 1910, we can see Bert Fortier's house (now the Dyrenforth house) on the left; on the right in the background is the Flanagan home. (Courtesy Steve Damon.)

CHOCORUA: The view is from the bridge over the Chocorua River looking east toward Madison. The Riverside Tearoom and Gift Shop sign says "Ice Cream and Cold Drinks." (Courtesy Steve Damon.)

CHOCORUA: A couple stands on the Narrows Bridge in 1886 overlooking Chocorua Lake with the Red Gables homestead in the background. The house still stands but the pagoda to the left is gone. Note how low the lake was at that time. Busy Route 16 now runs between the lake and the home. (Courtesy Tamworth Historical Society.)

TAMWORTH: This scenic *c.* 1905 view of Tamworth village shows the Waukaneto House and barn at center left; the large house to right is the Hannah Wiggin home at the four corners. To the left of the Wiggin place is the old brick schoolhouse. (Courtesy Charles Remick.)

WHITTIER: The fording place just west of the west lawn of the Will Smith (now the Karl Smith) place on old Route 25 was the original river crossing prior to building bridges. Harry Berry in the 1950s remembered: ". . . there used to be a road across river . . . and every summer they put a stringer piece there at the ford . . . You'd walk it to the field." Before the Smiths, the home was owned by many Remicks from Enoch to Mary. The barn in the picture still stands across the road; the house—hidden by trees—has been rebuilt after two disastrous fires. (Courtesy George Smith.)

CHOCORUA: James Pond, located off Fowlers Mill Road, is well known to many fishermen. In the 1950s Fred Hammond recalled: "Yes I have hunted around here. There were some cellar holes near James Pond. I don't think it was ever an inn but there was quite a little cleared land. I think the coach road went up through here." (Courtesy Steve Damon.)

TAMWORTH: The village square made for a tranquil scene at the turn of the century. The building at the right was the Willow Inn, and now serves as the town offices and the Tamworth Community Nurse Office. In the background at the left is Kimball's store—now the Barnstormers Theater. (Courtesy Tamworth Historical Society.)

WONALANCET: Gazing down Route 113A (a dirt road at that time) coming into the intervale from Sandwich, we see the beautiful Wonalancet Chapel across the field in the distance with the mountain range as a backdrop (see p. 22). (Courtesy Steve Damon.)

WONALANCET: Chinook Kennel was named after Arthur Walden's favorite sled dog. Walden trained the sled dogs used for the first expedition to the Antarctic with Admiral Byrd. Milt and Eva Seeley took over the kennels after Walden's retirement and moved the outfit to their place further down the appropriately named "Chinook Trail." The picture shows dog mobile rides in 1947 at the kennels. The buildings are now in private hands but a state historical plaque stands at the side of the road. (Courtesy Steve Damon.)

Eight
Et Cetera! Et Cetera! Et Cetera!

TAMWORTH: The first permanent minister in Tamworth village, Parson Samuel Hidden, at the time a recent Dartmouth graduate, was ordained in 1792 on this "Ordination Rock" by a council of six ministers. The monument erected in 1862 to commemorate this event was provided by a grandson who carried the same name. (Courtesy J. and M. Hidden.)

TAMWORTH: This pre-1902 gathering of ladies consisted of, from left to right: (front row) Susan Philbrook, Hannah Remick, Hannah Hatch Carr or Eliza Chesley, Harriet Remick, Maria Louisa Lincoln, Sarah Remick Hubbard, Susan Cook, and Harriet Seavy; (second row) Abigail Gilman Varney, Mary Swazey Banks, Mrs. William Hamilton Tilton, Lydia Beede Gilman Jackson, Lydia Merrill, and Miss White; (third row) Amanda Davis, Miss True, Miss Lincoln, and Sarah Davis; (back row) Ellen J. Gilman and Augusta Stevenson. (Courtesy Tamworth Historical Society.)

TAMWORTH: This photograph of a combined Women's Club and Onaway Club was taken in 1940. From left to right are: (front row) Mrs. Carle, Mamie Whiting, Ida Mahoney, Violet Huntress, Gussie Whipple, Eva Baker, Mrs. Sweet (the minister's wife), Sara Frances Kimball, and Elsie Hidden; (middle row) Florence Spaulding, Maybelle Farnum, Harriet Cartland, Mary Kimball, Frances Damon, Ginny Atkins, Clara Black, Marjorie Gregg, Laura Heald, and Sadie Stevens; (back row) Peggy Henderson, Tessie Henderson, Stella White, Helen Brett, Flora Mason, Elizabeth Buck, Ellen Bookholz, Laura Prescott, and Ethel Henderson Lord. (Courtesy Tamworth Historical Society.)

SOUTH TAMWORTH: This building was formerly owned by C.W. Whitehouse, and then Albion Hayford, with John Hayford as the blacksmith. It was located on the old River Road (now old Route 25). (Courtesy Tamworth Historical Society.)

TAMWORTH: Francis Cleveland snapped this photograph in the mid-1950s on the last day of work for Tamworth switchboard operators Mildred Wilkinson (on the left), Mabel Hidden (seated), and Jan Dearborn. "Dialing" had arrived. Mabel added some background: "For 'round the clock service the operator on duty was obliged to sleep on a cot beside the switchboard. Note the oil lamp in the upper left corner; if the power went off, the switchboard did not and a light to work by was necessary." (Courtesy J. and M. Hidden.)

WONALANCET: Arthur Walden stands with Chinook, the world-famous sled dog who sired a long line of Chinook dogs, went to the South Pole with Admiral Byrd's first expedition, and eventually died there (see p. 82). (Courtesy Elva Bickford.)

ALBANY: The Halfway House built by Jim Liberty was located quite appropriately halfway up Mt. Chocorua on the Liberty Trail (see p. 70). (Courtesy Steve Damon.)

OSSIPEE CORNER: The courthouse, built in the style of New England meetinghouses, was opened in 1840 and became the seat for the new Carroll County, also created that year. In 1856–57 brick wings were added. It burned in the destructive c. 1915 fire which destroyed buildings on the south side of the village, but was rebuilt in 1916. (Courtesy Steve Damon.)

OSSIPEE: The Carroll County Poorhouse, also called the Almshouse and the Carroll County Farm, was built in 1870. Previously, the poor were boarded in private homes for small amounts of money paid by the town, or were placed in local town poorhouses. (Courtesy Steve Damon.)

127

Acknowledgments

Our thanks to the following individuals and groups for the photographs used in this visual history of our three towns: from Albany—the Albany Historical Society, Ruth and George Morrill, and Elaine Wales; from Ossipee—the Ossipee Historical Society, Arletta Paul, and Beryl Kramer; and from Tamworth—the Tamworth Historical Society, the Cook Memorial Library, the Union Hall Association, Elva Bickford, David Bowles, Francis Cleveland, Nancy Coville, Florence Fortier, Barbara Fromm, John and Mabel Hidden, Ralph Raabe, Charles Remick, Judy Schibanoff, George Smith, Helen Steele, Lorraine Streeter, Millie Streeter, Kate Thompson, the Ulitz family, and last, but by no means least, we are indebted to Steve Damon for the many selections from his fabulous postcard collection.

Putting together this book required much research for the written information and the captions. We are grateful to the Cook Memorial Library for allowing us working space in their Genealogy and History Center and for the resources available for research. Besides the written material listed next, we are also thankful for the memories of some of our older fellow citizens: *Albany Recollections* by Perry, *Albany Bicentennial Observance* by Perry, *The Russell-Colbath House* by Leavitt and Croto, *Chocorua Peak House* by Nickerson, *Ossipee, N.H. 1785–1985* by Cook, *Early Ossipee: A Pictorial View 1976*, Elaine Wales' history of her family, *Carroll County History* by Merrill, *If Walls Could Speak* by McGrew, *Tamworth Recollections* by Hidden and Ulitz, *Tamworth Narrative* by Harkness, *Interviews of Mid-1950s* by Harkness, *History of Chocorua Public Library* by Davies and Smith, the Tamworth Old Home Week 1906 booklet, David Ruell's *A Guide to National Register Properties in the Lakes Region* and his Survey of Southern Carroll County Churches, and E. Eloise Beane's *History of Water Village*, et al.